T0006593

CRYING DRESS

CRYING DRESS

POEMS

CASSIDY McFADZEAN

ANANSI

Copyright © 2024 Cassidy McFadzean

Published in Canada in 2024 and the USA in 2024 by House of Anansi Press Inc.
houseofanansi.com

All rights reserved. No part of this publication may be reproduced or transmitted in any form or by any means, electronic or mechanical, including photocopying, recording, or any information storage and retrieval system, without permission in writing from the publisher.

House of Anansi Press is a Global Certified Accessible™ (GCA by Benetech) publisher. The ebook version of this book meets stringent accessibility standards and is available to readers with print disabilities.

28 27 26 25 24   1 2 3 4 5

Library and Archives Canada Cataloguing in Publication
Title: Crying dress : poems / Cassidy McFadzean.
Names: McFadzean, Cassidy, author.
Identifiers: Canadiana (print) 20230505597 | Canadiana (ebook) 20230505600 |
ISBN 9781487012588 (softcover) | ISBN 9781487012595 (EPUB)
Subjects: LCGFT: Poetry.
Classification: LCC PS8625.F35 C79 2024 | DDC C811/.6—dc23

Cover design: Greg Tabor
Cover image: Costume design for the *Triadic Ballet*, 1919.
Found in the Collection of Bauhaus-Museum Weimar.
Book design and typesetting: Lucia Kim

House of Anansi Press is grateful for the privilege to work on and create from the Traditional Territory of many Nations, including the Anishinabeg, the Wendat, and the Haudenosaunee, as well as the Treaty Lands of the Mississaugas of the Credit.

With the participation of the Government of Canada
Avec la participation du gouvernement du Canada   Canadä

We acknowledge for their financial support of our publishing program the Canada Council for the Arts, the Ontario Arts Council, and the Government of Canada.

Printed and bound in Canada

for Kourosh

CONTENTS

SUMMER

FALL

WINTER

CHAMBER MUSIC

Ringing in the year with brutalism and velour
Accidental accentual outfits

Show me a building with no facing

The sparrow begging for crumbs
rests inside the hollow of your chest

What does it mean to be vulnerable?
I don't disguise my raw materials

Sadness is present   Desire is present

Oversharing our worst selves
A ringing in the ears

I could live pressed against your body
like a bird or polished stone

Brutal in the same basic ways

GO SIT IN THE WHITE HOT

Before bed, I count teeth slipping out,
calculate bodies in the high-rise above

As a child, who comforted you
when you stirred from sleep?

Did you stand in the doorway,
watching softly snoring faces,

too terrified to step inside a room?
When I'm crying a little or a lot,

you run for me the white hot
You were flying home from Tehran

I was bleeding in the bathtub
at the start of the next decade

A toast to this and all other
odds and eclogues

Was it maggot or magnets?
Static or stagnant? No matter—

we cherished each fragment
clasped to our clavicles, tight

You visited the Tower of Silence
and returned with copper bracelets

I wore clinking down the aedicula,
songbird ghoori glazed ash-white

IN SPECTRE OF SALT

Teenage scars migrate from arm to bicep
Those clumps in the toilet   a heavy period
Playing my pussy's suppository pennywhistle
toast with sugar and drinking vinegar

We simmer a strawberry shrub
feel for the horn at the base of the neck
grown from this grotesque internet
Our future will be happy for now

Love that dissipates into a gradient of narcissism
Would you beg for your life? I don't run
to catch the bus, but cure the sweating sickness
with a cold shock response

Searching for a salt cave to slip into
Felt-hatted Russians in a wood stove sauna
their broom of fragrant birch branches
whipping our bodies омар red

KISSING THE ABYSS

I land on beast's knees   Bruised fruit

A body ripe with fermentation

Rotting to the core   The stench

of fallen apples   Put out to pasture

Loose as chartreuse   Take a gander

Lose my way in the wayzgoose alley

Palpitations trigger hard races

Pinfire blood pressure   An indentation

Depression is the tops   I sat rock bottom

Knee-deep in gemstones   Cutting teeth

on my own two feet   Tenor subterranean

Vamoose to a distant land   Dissociate

Can't swallow this lump in my throat

Cold shower's no water off my back

Body shocked I pare myself   Slip

out of skin   Another bump on this toad

Despair pairing   Fingernail blackened

I'm smashing   Dressed for distress

Reel me in   Each breath a bonfire

Stick a pitchfork in me   Heaven-scent

POND

Edge of parabola, darkening
The crater filled with turquoise,
imprint in the earth, a glassy eye

Input zero cameras; input infinite
cameras   Early morning glass
breaking exists before dishes,

predates ceramics, an oval
seared in flesh   Pale yellow
tissue re-forms, delicate

as a wriggling maggot   Low
drum of slamming doors,
work boots running down

concrete stairs   Fitful freight
elevator, figure jostling
the handle of a door; a hand's

sudden clasping of shoulder
Ice exhales across the surface,
creaking as you turn

FERAL PARENTERAL

Antennae tunneled in the circuit board
Poppy seeds scattered on linoleum,

the desk, the floor, carried on the backs
of arthropods, the kidney's honeycomb ridges

Microcameras obscured in track lighting
A static channel   The garden exhumed

Latex scraped from seedpod and milky white
I swallow the thrush's song

Bathtub musky with Stachybotrys
spores released from slimy heads

Benign aphthae biopsy   Fungal breeding
dead moll's fingers swelling from rotting trunks

Hydrogen peroxide scoured my breasts
Deep-cleaned tinea versicolour's fallow deer,

poisoned on false morels we foraged
Threads of mycelium transmitting tree signals

I speak from the crater of my scalloped tongue
An irritating sliver   This fibreglass rash

Tannin-dyed the sclera of my corneal infiltrates
immunocompromising chronic affliction

Saprobic fungi devoured leaf litter
Digging through discarded ornamental cultivars,

the lotus-eater's cuticles caked with dirt
Inflicted the zebra finch's induced stammer

Flypaper flecked with black   Belated birthday streamers
Opium pods boiling on the kitchen stove

SPURIOUS EMISSIONS

The building grates above us,
a voice box grinding back and forth

Sound ricochets bags of breaking
glass down the garbage chute

It's not the scurrying that wakes,
but the pounding on metal doors

A ghost whiplashes my body
Footsteps that follow and stop

Ever bracing for a door to burst open
and throw back the sheets

Cornered by a shadow sirocco
Pulling out all its false starts

Sooner I suss out the colour sucked
Psyche's better off disembodied

My peripheral vision flickers
coaxing a noise that doesn't end

ENFILADE TERRIBLE

Cold air cured my melancholia
I keep losing bobby pins down the drain

I run back to the apartment
to clip barrettes into my hair

Botero's adult babies
Sucking all the air / heir / err

An elephant in the room
is something you can only *feel*

I spend my days pacing the parquet floor
To really understand you

I need to read *Junkspace*
Affectation, corruption: a flower held and seen

Michaelangelo buried his own forgeries
Sleeping Cupid in the vineyard

The twisting limbs of Laocoon
Wing-deep in the Winter Palace

Painting our trompe l'œil's room
within a room within a room

A BREACH OF FRESH AIR

Sometimes you confuse me with other women
scanning our heads in a crowd
I'm not particularly photogenic
The camera makes me self-conscious
I never learned to pose

Wind fills my puffer on the roundabout
I become airborne on the walk over
Skywriting: a classical artform
The professor thwarted foodborne illness
but fell victim to zoonotic disease

The randomizer gestures from offstage
A memory misplaced:
never arriving, but the waiting is the same
Unmoored   As if all of childhood's a dream
or simply never was

OUT-OF-BODY EXPERIMENT

It's tiring when a piece of yourself
drifts outside your body

If I think hard enough
is the sum of my life cerebral?

I left my capacity for tenderness
in the mountains

My subconscious performs
a ritual to banish the darkness

When did it first present itself,
this condition?

A snail cast in bronze
My body suspended between neon walls

It burns the scented candle,
stares at a tarot

A cord in my chest
stops my torso from floating away

It tugs at the end of a string,
this helium animal

tied to a child's wrist
You always know just what to seance

Me in the next room reading:
dull, nagging pain

SEVERANCE

Winter Sundays feel particularly apocalyptic

The weekend spent narrating each terrifying angel

There was a time we could have gone back but that time has passed

Wearing the selfsame clothes until pilled and threadbare

One day my heel stuck to the wooden floor

A coin-sized hole let the feeling in

cold and unfamiliar as a kiss

or a pebble stuck in the heel of my shoe

This is what you've become to me and me to you

The cut-out less real than the empty space

There was a time we could have tried again,

which we did for a while and then we didn't

An omnipresent struggle with objectivity

Putting on last winter's coat to find

the gloves that, missing all this time, no longer fit

The last of intimacy teased out

as if water from the stone, obstinate

BRIDLE PATH WALK OF SHAME

In the Uber to your parents' house
I roll my eyes at myself

Are there people in your life
who remind you of your worst self?

You like the angle of my lenses
like I like doughnuts and rebar

I lick the salt under your nails—
we can't have sweetness all the time

Ugo Rondinone's three neon boulders
precarious in the teardrop drive

That oil painting in the foyer—
we suspect it's haunted

The previous owners absconded
with the doorknobs and sconces

We burn the cursed Marseilles deck
We swallow pomegranate seeds

Two creatures buzzing
with tenderness and brutality

Let's not speak of Ronnie's
We inspect each other's teeth

Each of our midnights in the bathtub
Always say yes, never say when

In the morning we take the wrong bus,
scurrying when it comes again

WIN BEFORE YOU BEGIN

Is it any use ...

Clasping the camp bed and the cloak

we walked down to St. Alban's Square

The alley smelled like onion rings
        grease traps never cleaned

Bobby socks dyed with avocado skins

Bobby pins crosshatching baby hairs

Carrying a Frida Kahlo pillow
        salvaged curbside

A future brimming with succour and succotash
        Voices shouting from the sports bubble

This walk feels good with the steeple ahead

resting our crowns on a holly bush

Did you see the figure in the window
        of the manse? *Nah,*

it was just a spectre in the rec room
      coattails hanging in the corner

Walked from the barracks back to town
      clutching a cushion

When the crystal clattered in the night
      was it just the wind?

IT WORMS MY HEART

We have reached the time of squeezing

hunkered down for honeymoon season

dressed in our matching puffers

You like driving with your hand on the stick

Would you still love me if I were a snake?

SSENSE for seven months' sobriety

I got you and the goblins (goblets)

Watching Kiarostami to distract me

Sick to my stomach I bought some stupid shit:

seersucker, threads pinched together

I pluck the feathers from your coat

No photographing Rubens's *Medusa*

Chaotic good for psychic ills

Inside the lines of our historiated initial

we burrow together like two puffins

rubbing our bills close

JUST LIKE I LIKE

The last tuft of winter:
an icicle grew from the garret

A lore   A loon
eking out terrors

Our nibs opining at the head,
nozzles clogged with deposits

That these youths dare seethe!
An unexamined knack for preening

Burst ducts birthed this deadly hornet,
withered uvula into viola

Raisin-royal, a goose at Kew Gardens
wandered this eulogy   A gas

Nevertheless mourning,
a pair of nuzzling ermines

settled near the testing site
Cursed image   wriggling at the core

On our islet of quarks,
acorns ever knocking into jars

BOOK OF OURS

Reviewing our shared lexicon

Ours   A propositional architecture

distracted neither by heat

nor the changing of seasons

but dried peaches and aromatic tea

Our rations dwindling   Hours dithered away

Each distant corner of the house we share

The point is mute   Sunlight sequestered

The purely ornamental string chorus

which sings of nothing but its pleasure

in singing for the pleasure   Purely

SPRING

TENDER PERENNIAL

You say to daydream
of squirrels or bees   Creatures
that swim or leap

Murmuring in our moosh language
I want to live on an island and dig
for fiddleheads   Chew their whorls

You part the curtains   Tell me
it's nice to keep a little light
for my noonday dreaming

Shoulder season   We cook
lentils and split peas   Veering
into hide-and-boo-seek

Caught in the blue and green
I don't want to loose you
Lease you   Lessen you

At twilight we sing together
See ya   Until wind-paired
we sleep

NURSERY

You know it's nice to sit in the clover

The man holding a squirming baby

calls me over from the attic window

A brass band playing on somebody's lawn

I've killed every plant I've ever grown

In St. Alban's Square we sat and ate paper

You called love *a feeling of sacrifice*

and enchantment at the same time

We took down my six sets of curtains

The flashing lights kept us awake

examining Uno's angles in the lobby

We walked behind the train tracks

to a parking lot   A strobing lantern

illuminating a car with no one inside

THE CROWN WAS AN END STOP

We want to burn in the flames
those who misread our pasts

We can forage some herbs maybe
forge the path to intimacy

A blemish on my shoulder,
porcelain chipped away

A pigeon struck my head at Kipling
The train dry-heaves beside the platform

You point out lines on my face:
a smile held in parentheses

You called architecture
a detour to the human

We had such trouble focusing,
unable to envision our futures

until we tricked ourselves into living,
each day's exercise in amnesia

ANIMAL FANCY

Befriend a garden variety of trees
Identify birds by their calls
We lick the nectar from bees' knees

a tiny sweetness dissolving under our tongues
You slather lotion and smell evergreen:
You're a garland   you're an effigy

Sprouted lentils I could not keep from wilting
Poppies dropping petals from the desk
I dreamed we careened off a cliff

I asked if you believe in angels
You said you believe in putti—
that they should be placed on buildings

When I can't sleep from the ghost knocking
at our closet door   I imagine myself
as a mushroom releasing a cloud of spores

PIER EVIL

We travelled all day to say hello to the ocean

It was only a plane, then a bus, and then a ferry, and then a bus

The flower our goal

Seated on the pier, wasn't it romantic

when we watched the podcast about colours?

Nothing blue in nature but pebbles

Calling six months' sobriety a cleanse

It's not a problem; it's a condition

Sweet as treacle   seated under the trestle   A suite of trellises

We are making flowers speak squeezing the petals together

An onomatopoeic language / words that evoke a feeling

In Farsi the past is cruel

We watched an animal's pelt disappear into clover

Glimpses of future children as captive listeners

A flower called maymoon

The most interesting part of architecture is the non-functioning

We crushed the veneer of a robin's egg

antirrhinum majus

and left when the crowd started chanting

TREE / TREE / TREE

GLASS PAVILION

I watered the tulips that wilted overnight
When we sleep in the loft the bad dreams dissipate
Not that it's not bad   but like it's no big deal
Your subconscious carries a cumulus over us
Slanted walls whisper exhausted prophecies

We were stirring lentils and reading Pinter
Birthday guests rode the freight elevator
Abandoned houseplants   pre-stretched canvases
We locked ourselves out on the rooftop
knocking for the ceramicist to let us in

In the night my fears crystallize into daggers
My parched tongue wants for water
The factory window   gradient blue
A curled spider falls from my hair
I dreamed I wrote a poem in the shape of a star

SEEDING SUNSETS

Spring chicken   Look at you vicious
Our skin heating when we lean
into the concrete's thermal mass

That man is searching for a cigarette
or baby bird beneath the metal grating
It's not a parlance   it's a dynamic

Time perceived only through entropy
its passing otherwise indiscernible
You have to wreck it to feel it

Get down to our hands and knees
Time is a concert   When we fuck
a tiny feather floating to your thigh

NEW BUCOLICS

Filling in each other's wrinkles

with a dropper of peptides

I'm a plant   you need to water

I hold your feet to the fire

and wake from nightmares

to a pink sky   Early morning

I cloister in your cavity

the space between your ribs

You comfort and calm me

A landscape   like Iceland

The sound flowers make:

their tiny roots amplified

SOBER MOMENT

Writing a love letter in poison ivy
You're in one nostril out the other

Bedsheets a damp apparition
hanging from the door hinge

The more fractal our heartbeats the homier
Exhale dramatically through your nose

Gave away my laundry money
All money is dirty money

I walk through blue and white acrylic
to see how far our footsteps travel

Hoarding hunks of malachite
I'm wearing the apiarist's gold satin jumper

embroidered with bees and flowers
and a matching mesh-wire mask

FRETFUL

This disproportionate   spilling over

It comes as a pain that wakens in the night

To bind (properly, with a hoop or ring)

I supine-twisted out of my spine

and still couldn't escape my fretting

Of architecture   A ceiling adorned

with carved or embossed work

composed of intersecting lines in relief

Of animals (now only small)   To eat and devour

It gnaws or consumes from within

Erosion (now rare)

To rub or chafe, torture by wearing away

A canker   reddened sore   decaying spot

(in the wood of a bow or arrow, in a hair)

The tongue prods the ulcer in the back of the mouth

A figure formed by two bendlets, dexter and sinister

Weaving an ornament of jewels or flowers

in a network of lace

A net of gold or silver embroidery

Of water   Agitated, troubled, broken into waves

A breach or passage made by the sea

A strait

WORRYWORT

I pull a card and make a wish
Sipping from horseshoe decanter—
I must have licked a toad

The scalpel slices flesh
Silver nitrate for the growth,
matchstick for the tissue

The flesh cauterized   Singing
defiant speech from the tip
of my blackened tongue

Three stitches hold me in
Waiting for a cryptic message:
It's exactly as we expected

The garlic clove's insides:
a remedy imprinted with
the signature of its scourge

The root of it remained
Virus feeding on mutant genes
Stuttering Philomela

I spill my gut feeling
A voice on a screen insisting
The light in you is all I see

BRIDGE

I must confess to flickers of envy
Will it happen for us one day?

I was out in the scary world
meeting people I had met before

You said: peace, tranquility, and love
are not my priorities

What's the solution—
a good slogging?

If so, I surrender
Lately, everything wearies:

That you prefer happy baby
to toppling tree

Your suggested title: *You haven't told me
I'm beautiful once today*

I expected heaviness
I expected terror

In an evil hour
I pressed my feet against the floor

and found the weight of my body
not too much to bear

LAKE BABY

Maybe there's a place we can swim

a lake or creek   lagoon

to lower our bodies into and bathe

Could we make something happen?

Luring in me   like the fish

we witnessed deepthroating an eel

unaware the clip depicted the carp

devoured from the inside out

Didn't your family used to farm wind

in a space outside the city?

We could stand under the turbines

as the blades graze our faces

Maybe there's a gorge or quarry

somewhere we can find   Time

still to sink into a salt cave

shining with stalactite

GILDING THE LILY

Someone put glasses on Gwendolyn

Her bust, a makeshift lost and found

I come to the statue with sparkling water

Tiny spiders dotting my skin

cherry angioma   I sit on a bench

to get a break from the ghosts

Spiders on the railing furiously weaving

in the storm   in a fury

The eldest caught between panes

of the window above my desk

Webs adhere to my phone screen

after I drop it on the balcony

startled by your presence

To languish, in language

conquered by all I can't contain

HELIOTROPE

Standing in the sun like crocuses
with hair we cut ourselves
We take turns with the smelling salts

inspect our toes for outgrowths
I comb the virus out of your hair
The front-facing camera's dysmorphia

I wore *an unfamiliar smile*
nostalgic for a moment even as it unfolds
The bud of a tadpole in cupped palms

prodding the boundaries of skin
Or pink and yellow poppies
antennae bobbing over the desk

We sit in Christie Pits, a landfill
of dropped petals covered in sod
Nothing better than frozen mud

All your life trying to recapture a feeling
and failing   Trying and failing
to surrender yourself to the sun

LITTLE ISLAND

My beloved eats sliced oranges
wrapped in lavashak

I'm sobbing at the concert behind the pair
who aren't mother and son

My mask soaks up my tears
I'm just so happy to be here

singing Lucinda Williams's "Like a Rose"
I never stutter when I'm alone

We were two guinea pigs on Little Island
darting into one another's fur

The art of back-scratching
a certain architecture or ballet

As a child I spent hours searching
for a word that rhymes with orange

The doctor said my cervix
was like a tiny mouth, smiling

I mistook my nipple
for a pebble at the beach

It's no longer smiling, she said,
sliding the speculum into me

BIRTHDAY SONNET

I dreamed the backyard was filled with lilacs,
fragrant and delicate clusters of white
When I woke, I thought my mother would write me
from a land where flowers are always in bloom
Isn't it nice being a person who inspires pink
bouquets? Carnations, tulips, peonies …
Maybe every poet wants to be a ballerina,
marvelling at bodies contorting in space

Tiered by flying back and forth all year,
these mooshes are not meant for travails
I wish I was there to lick your earlobe
I'll always be the egg on your iPhone screen
We will be each other's guardian angels
We will protect each other's peace

SUMMER

WHICHING OUR

Fortune distributes boons and woes
banishing those who demand too many boons
So marks a third of my life   which seems a sliver
the further I slither from it
and all the silver baubles are shaken down

It was neither ham-fisted nor pussyfooted
yet I felt its heaviness   And and and
even as I moved through its corridors
There were riches and sorrows   sorrows and riches
The song's the same   a chorus repeats

A night fretful with worries
from Old English *wyrgan*   to strangle
seize by the throat and tear
So it goes   the hangman in my throat
What music embedded   in its skipping track

FIELD OF MARS

I crawled out of the bramble
berserker waking from a nightmare
Following my bumbling shadow
rabid bozo   plucking burrs from my hair

On sniffing unscented candles in Zara Home ...
preteens twirling ponytails in the Summer Garden
I sit in the back with the boys and vomit
my brain's gyroscope gone kaput

On not visiting the grave of the ersatz soldier ...
time-travelled lilacs in my mother's portico
My building smells like trash   I'm ovulating
A bee in my bonnet in the crotch of the fig tree

DERANGED HYDRANGEA

Caught in wanton wanting
sipping stinging nettle tea
we flatten our days,
find petals light-bent, hydrangeas
beaten into the chesterfield
Will our children brandish sticks?

The tin of tennis balls opening
with a hiss   Hydration's
a cold one I no longer sip,
neon whirring across the court
We counted down from ten
but you're the first to reach eleven

And another one beyond the fence
Next time we'll bring our own net
duck under the parked Corvette
Echoes of future children asking
Baba, can we take the Porsche?
Can we find a rose bush all Saturday

Stopping at a bough to ask
What blossoms are these?
Moosh, this is an apple tree
Still, you insisted rose, invoking
little Rosie, Rosa, Rosaline …
Call it a comeback, the decade

came out swinging and roaring
We came to abhor our arborists
who planted only male trees
blowing pollen along the promenade
Oh what fruits we might have eaten
What air we might have breathed

FUN FACT OR CONSPIRACY THEORY

Drinking lead in the tap water

Another pipe burst   Tree roots

    digging into foundation

When the city shuts the water off

we practise scrying in cloudy bowls

    Is a tree architectural?

The man who hated the Eiffel Tower

    so much he lived inside it

Good or bad you're making yourself the subject

    of your own lie

It's very pure   the harmless narcissist

A horse that's stung by a wasp

    and doesn't know why it's running

The constant, directionless sense of panic

some artists feel most of the time

    uncertain of their worth

Embodied experience prevents you from seeing yourself

I don't believe in god but I'm god-fearing

Sitting in the tower   ever trying

Tell me you're going to enjoy it

this life of making

TAKING OFF WITH THE LUTE

No backflips / Only frontflips

Trauma dissolved into water memory

Eating stone fruit by the diving board

I should hook my amygdala to an amp

and drag race down the avenue

Seven times pleasure / seven times shame

The man in a reflective vest

on a scooter blasting its incessant song

I could sing along to noise pollution

falling victim to motion success

Drink you under the water table

like a prairie lily / for Italy

A flute carved from earth's oldest oak

Broker / warbler / thief

MAMMALIAN DIVING REFLEX

For those unlearned self-soothers

not lax or slipshod, negligent

through some failing of moral character—

but passed over   as in overlooked

otherwise obstructed from its truths

Did Deor dunk his face in a vat of rainwater

after the Heodenings cancelled him?

Reciting our scanty mantras

we, like dolphins, immerse our faces

seer / suck / sooth / say

Water caresses skin above the cheekbones

and just below the eye sockets

Think of seals   otters   muskrats

Like shir o shekar, we're milk and sugar

nature calming what nurture neglects

I should have been a pair of ragged calls

The cold water calms the siren's shrieking

Of the bathroom's mascara-flecked basin

quiet shock / spelunker diving / breath-cached

Seal man   signet   selkie

SHADOW RACING

Ergot poisoning put Saint Anthony's fire

in our Hieronymus Bosch

Snails, like raindrops on tall grasses

beneath the creeping funierice service

our shadows tracing landscape

Thousands of ants laminar flowed

down the mountain   Insect dinner rush

Is it fireworks or Mount Etna erupting?

The pathway green in UV

We gave ourselves colour-blind tests

Discovered on the breakwater

protrusions like reddened cervixes

dozens of tiny crabs scurrying

Kourosh cleaned his shirt

in the medieval laundry

and dreamed I was possessed

A changeling hovered over me

the twin I ate in the womb

L'Hypnol   Le mortherbe

I lost my footing waking

in the middle of the sea

WELL WE'LL WELL

Fluting's the only feature distinguishing
columns from stone / Barricade
the cult's secret worship room

Baroque is curved surfaces
Colloquially, anything embellished
Gothic / a broken arch

Madonnas glare in the alleyway
Giant mural of Apollo and Daphne:
pagan crime prevention scheme

A covered cistern / Living my best lie
Last year's fruits rotting the agora
Been all rain since we left, babe

How many colours can a snail see?
It's not sexual; it's structural
Travel, an exercise in slowing time

The temple embellished in polychrome
Terracotta Gorgon mask / Flouting
my *luxurious self-taught stammer*

MUTTER OF PEARL

The painting of Silenus was satyrical

Why do you write such blasphemy?

>It was Oberon, Titania, Puck, &c.

>>*Stagnated, an active verb*

Did you catch my toppling tree?

I'm painting in a shade only tetrachromatics can see

>It was birds, fish, reptiles, some mammals …

We stigmatized stigmata

took to pretense and subterfuge

>>*Rot, a generative process*

Worst thought: dead-end idea

Our lives were two split-screens before you entered

We burned the effigy

>>*It was strong, resilient, and iridescent*

>>*Mother, dregs or scrum concreted*

The sound of your voice became vibrations

thrumming against my body

ENERGY EXCHANGE

Where is the river that was here?

I would very much like to see it

the shirtless man yells in Bickford Park

Hours after leaving   happy as Lazarus

I pulled the cord at the side of the building

Watched my grief give out from underneath

like the elevator clicking as it climbs each floor

finally giving in to free fall   We fought

I walked through the Annex at 4 a.m.

A woman clad in white floated toward me

the fabric of her track pants   illuminated

The next morning you trimmed my hair

on the balcony   Cut rotten peaches

The knife slicing through the softened pits

easy-peasy   Last summer one such core

housed a black hard-shelled insect

An earwig in the pit of my nectarine

Impulses driven by base desires

We had our fill of mourning music

and stood in the ear of Dionysus

wriggling   I had to look away

Can we visit the bird that dive-bombs

pedestrians in Liberty Village?

The park littered with face masks

Mounds of potato chips   alluvial

We restored the warm fuzzies

A caterpillar in my brain   Ferrofluid

on glass with a magnet underneath

CALYX OF HELD

It was shoulder season when you cradled

my crown in your hands like a purple

echinacea with a damaged stalk

Oh baby flower, you need to fix that stem

on your head   I was a mouthful of water

you held in cupped hands   My spine,

climbing ivy   I was wisteria hanging,

cosmos, pollen collected under the nail

of your thumb   I was blue as snow

glory   Amaryllis with a broken stake,

asters strewn on Annex walkways   I was

pincushions, veronica, rain-heavy stonecrop

You pressed your lips to my forehead

and held the kiss, sipping me, I thought

GARDEN FOLLY

We were beating your carpet

in the backyard with a plastic broom

Dust mites dispersing in clouds

like the steam from my tea made visible

its particles rising to the aether

All things suited to their places:

vapor belongs to the heavens   water to the earth

In this way, our bodies belong to each other

In the bathtub   in the bed

You were a mouse in the factory

manufacturing a series of measuring devices

like the gas valves outside our Uno Prii

A spring inside the meter stops its overheating

And other mechanisms I couldn't comprehend

my framework of thought medieval

We were seated on the grass   on the greenery

In a secret courtyard of standing water

forking cubes of melon into our mouths

You rolled your eyes when I asked about *deliberate mistakes*

The factories you stood to inherit:

the possibilities of bark-based polyurethane

Our futures slotted together like spoons

On the balcony   on the chesterfield

We placed the carpet beneath your sister's table

and lay us in its garden

SO THIS IS WHAT A BED OF ROSES FEELS LIKE

How can we nip this in the bud?

It has already grown into a beautiful tree

Sipping rosé, you pointed out

our shadows made a heart shape

in the rose garden, like the ending

of every *Powerpuff Girls* episode:

a hypnotic, pulsating beam

Moments earlier, I found you

fingering the centifolia:

a rose with a hundred frilled petals

It was nice to sniff the hybrids

that in April hadn't bloomed,

still wrapped in burlap and rope

On my deathbed, I hope I'm not cold

Seated by the fountain, we watched

turtles swimming in a pond of lily pads,

posited which garden housed the highest

concentration of happy souls

Later, a ladybug climbed the curtains

like a blood spot we positioned

in the atrium of your paper home

VEIL OF CASHMERE

A man is quacking at a swan
as steel drums play somewhere behind

James says get the tears out
before the meeting. Good advice

Last night I dreamed I was drinking
a glass of cider and ice with a straw

In the ravine, I felt a moment
of connection with the trees

I moved a turtle off the trail,
Its spring-loaded limbs kicking

from heavy shell, contorting its head
as it hissed. It wanted to bite me

That would have been alright
I blinked and flashes

filled the forest, sparks leaping
from the end of a magician's wand

Things vanish quickly:
the bird inside the tree trunk,

the last text message
my mother ever sent

In the Vale of Cashmere,
I sat surrounded by fireflies,

listening to a harpist playing
over the cacophony

and on the walk home
came across a peacock,

a rabbit, a family of raccoons,
and my friend Irene

Another lightning bolt—there
now I'm gone

FALL

GERM

Gnawing on pink ladies,

we swallow the seed

that enters this world

with all it requires

Dispersal   if not by wind

then water or beak

One hooked barb

caught on the nape

of my neck   I called to you

to pull it out   in the shower

Clawing at my body

panicked at the thought

of a tick burrowing

in my skin   its head

embedded like a follicle

You washed my hair

discovered in the suds

a tightly coiled burr

or wooden spring

Maybe it was a seed

that found us eating apples

under the trees   Washing

our feet in the water

cloudy with silt

Less a mirror   merely

a dried-out tendril

carrying nothing

but the memory

of its reaching

KNOCK ON WOOD

When I'm on top   something
pops off like a dandelion
Tulip pods in the living room
Cavy popcorning in the sun

How fun it is to educate ourselves
instead of working like little thieves
When I smile, you say I resemble
a mechanical devil at the theme park

Walking a street with no sidewalk
Ugly houses but nice trees
At night   branches scratching glass
sing like an animal clawing inside

METAPHYSICAL TRUST ISSUES

No one can explain how sand dunes

communicate   Why planes stay in the air

Most theories can't account for low-pressure zones

Even Newton's third law falls short

between drag and thrust, weight and lift

You're much more superstitious than religious

Turning tree bark into polyurethane

Material engineering a kind of alchemy

Ever having fun in public

I'm camera-shy   A particle unwatched

in the double-slit experiment

It's part physics, part atomic loneliness:

The fear that when I lean against a wall

the wall won't return my touch

SPLENDID COIL

At the combination Department of Classics /

Club Monaco we roll clay into ropes

Making snakes   the most basic technique

All things come from earth

Wedges shaped into a cup / a bowl / a vase

Gracia likes to preserve her finger marks

tells me not to be afraid of the clay

I like sinking my hands into it, playing

with a shape already hardening under my nails

I'm so tired these days   Can I come home

and cry, rest my head on your chest? It's okay

if I don't make a vessel to fire and glaze

Anything I shape simply slipping away

BARRED FROM THE BALLET

Take me to *Swan Lake*

Nostalgic for sipping

dipping in and out

You call me bard

Waking early / already

hard at work

at the ceramics factory

Every day we click

a random place to visit

Yesterday a villa

in Italy   Today rain

clouds in Brazil

At night

I kiss the soft skin

behind your neck

Painting the screen

with pomegranate

POEM WITH NO PERSPECTIVE

This rose is all sniffed out, lost its smell

Lingering heart note of despair

Is there a reason you didn't grieve the loss when it occurred?

the grief facilitator asks on the phone

Find me in the leaves   Dissociating

I am writing a poem with no perspective

I often lose it   Catastrophize

A body walking at an angle towards me

Abrasive to my aura   This psychic irritant

I have to remember the dead rat under golden leaves

Its delicate fur has already startled twice

Wearing my fluffy lilac coat

Made of clown-wig polyester

Playing the fool   I like fruit that is dusty

Not polished in the rock tumbler

I occasionally feel the urge to upend my life

Walking past a dive bar   Vague desire to indulge

I am writing a poem with no prospects

The tag warns KEEP AWAY FROM FIRE

Rebecca's concerned as I nestle against the heater

It's important to feel others are invested in your life

Chilly autumn evenings where it's nice to go inside

and inhale the heat of the furnace   Just caught

childhood whiff of tinsel on incandescent bulb

Clementine wrapped in green paper   Rotting

in a cardboard box in the front hallway

Grief pangs before the peristyle

Feeling mournful in my fluffy coat

Crying in the park due to memory

Wanted damage / so I damaged me / some

I'm a lonely person   but I like it that way

On the loop of Prospect Park

I feel at my core alone in the world

You wonder if the poet likes the bad feeling

or is just expressing it   Should I shed

the narratives I tell myself about myself

Maybe I should live closer to nature

Deep down I suspect I deserve this violence

All my life waiting for it to unfold

THE FALLS

You've never seen me on such a giant bed

In the edge of it   a room with a view

You booked two without caring

Tapping bathroom fixtures to establish

if metal or plastic   The Falls were majestic

We wanted to build a temple to their indifference

We should return this place to the elements

Canals instead of power stations and galleries

Learning from Las Vegas   duck vs. decorated shed

Intuit hauntings on sketched-out blocks

A city of crematoriums and tourists in pajama pants

Teleport your house to a field of tumbleweeds

Garbage bins dotting lot after empty lot

I dreamed of bleeding in the jacuzzi   distraught

And in the morning we woke to light

golden and good on the falling water

STORM KING

Peasants of this land build massive sculptures

to honour their king   For when he is pleased he shows mercy

and when displeased he rouses a hurricane

At the end of our trip it was supposed to rain but didn't

We approached *The Wavefield* but evaded its waves

and lay by a stone wall where I read to you "Mending Wall"

At home I bathed in the green copper water

Asked what you were building and you said *context*

We should think of each day as having twelve rounds

I'm tired of feeling things in my body   like ions

All the apartment's doorknobs have been removed

the last tenant afraid of being locked inside

Fear that manifests as compulsion   Where is the feeling

I used to have (that life was taking place)

ELEPHANT TOOTH

You brought tulips

because when they droop

they droop elegantly

The dentist said the root

curled in my gums delicately

The year all our bad luck

coalesced like cloudberries

rising from their stalks

In a world you no longer inhabit

I listen to a voice inside myself

singing a song at a lower decibel

singing its quieter song

BIRD PEOPLE

Can I still muster a sense of joy, wonder, curiosity?

When I was a rising character in another's world

I overheard a father telling his son:

Back in my day people didn't travel very normally

When I'm blue I go and see the bird feeders

The crowd photographing nuthatches and brown creeper

A girl breathing very heavily   that is me

Various pine species enclosed in steel cages

Did you feel a greater vitality in childhood?

How might one arouse enthusiasm for life once again?

No one shares in my nostalgia

The blue smear of acrylic affixed to concrete

outside my former quarters

To be a peripheral character in certain circles

A man screeching as a rat skirts between his legs

When sauerkraut was *victory cabbage*

A certain duplicity

The shovel that, clearing the field, chips itself on stone

Over time the edges of my teeth become jagged

from grinding against themselves in the night

How I injured my spirit pecking at its form

Or was I always of the world and its detritus

DON'T BASK IN THE PARABOLA

Whiplash from Forest Hill to Flatbush

I missed the mountains of trash

Riding the bus to Soho House

a lady warned me not to sit in the spit,

a red paint chip on blue plastic

The ocean is never kitsch   You tried

to teach me the meaning of aramesh:

comfort, peace of mind, tranquility

You insist protégés always fail

Someday is not a day of the week

When does the terror go away?

Even a rat knows when it's sleeping

with vermin   From Governor's Island

to another island, it's hard to find

your footing on shaky ground

YOU HAVE ME KISS THE DAHLIAS

When we leave, the next tenants

keep the curtains closed

We didn't mind who observed

our bathroom patterns

Darting from the bedroom

across the hardwood in the night

You were drawing houses

I was barefoot in the moonlight

None of the kiwis or avocados

we bought have ripened

When we return I forget our rituals

Saturday mornings in tatters

Ask me what's *anti-gone*

You dreamed you made me

Olivier salad which is salad Olivieh

The room looks brighter

with these forty-dollar flowers

CRYING DRESS

I said you could trace thought processes
like a series of intersecting bridges
imagining each fragment opening up the text

You called it *Piranesian*   Corridors
leading back to the point of origin
teasing a web with a *not* at its center

Later I unwrapped a dress your sister told you
to gift me when you were certain you loved me
My crying dress   its ribbons of blue, red, green

You called it *Triadic*   Oskar's ballet
Spoken word as directives   Love as action
The movement of a body in space   geometric

UNO PRII FAN CLUB

We wandered our way to a far-flung Uno Prii
Seven stars in the centre of rounded windows
I dreamed I could take pictures of things on earth
and show them to you wherever you were
I crouched in the sun with the lavender and the bees
and clicked as the creatures turned their tiny faces
Kourosh peeled a scrap of bark from a tree
Squirrels darted under the reddening leaves

There are so many ravines left to explore
When we leave, where does consciousness travel?
We channeled the magical seven storeys
The load felt lighter in our segment of world
You're on the other end of the viewfinder
the building shining in afternoon light

THE DEAD END IS STILL WORTH SEEING

Let's not loosen our heads

We should linger more in public squares

Having a good day in bad highlights

We're two animals in a strange room

Accusing the other of playing dumb

with ourselves and with the world

At the convention centre, art confronts

its commercial self, its least heroic state

The patterned glass reduced bird deaths 90%

You walked in Starbucks and asked for comfort tea

Comforter, where, where is your comforting?

SoulCycle's moment of silence for 9/11

Trace all weird feeling to atmospheric pressures

Our canvases hiding all this time behind plaster

Overheard at the museum: *What does capricious mean?*

Why is there blue cork in your hair?

The elaborate dream my mother faked her death:

she'd been swimming all this time in Texas

NOTES

"Spurious Emissions" is a term in radio communication for unintended signals, or noise.

In "Enfilade Terrible," "feel" is a near-homophone for فیل, which means "elephant" in Farsi.

"A Breach of Fresh Air" was written after seeing Anne Carson's "Lecture on the History of Skywriting" at University of Toronto's John H. Daniels Faculty of Architecture, Landscape, and Design.

In "Tender Perennial," "moosh" translates to "mouse" and is a term of endearment in Farsi; "see ya" is a near-homophone for سیاه, which means "black" in Farsi.

In "Pier Evil," "goal" is a near-homophone for گل, which means "flower" in Farsi; "maymoon" or میمون means monkey and refers to the monkey flower (snapdragon in English); "past" is a near-homophone for پست and refers to someone who is ignoble or cruel.

"Glass Pavilion" refers to Bruno Taut's Glass Pavilion.

"Field of Mars" borrows "the crotch of the fig tree" from Sylvia Plath.

"Mammalian Diving Reflex" misquotes T. S. Eliot.

"Well We'll Well" borrows a line from *Brideshead Revisited.*

"Mutter of Pearl" references William Blake's "Oberon, Titania and Puck with Fairies Dancing."

"Poem with No Perspective" borrows three lines from Graham Foust's "There. There, There."

"The Falls" references the architectural theory of the duck vs. decorated shed in Denise Scott Brown, Robert Venturi, and Steven Izenour's *Learning from Las Vegas.*

"Crying Dress" was written after reading Heather Christle's *The Crying Book* and references Oskar Schlemmer's *Triadic Ballet.*

"Uno Prii Fan Club" and a few other poems reference Uno Prii's Toronto high rises.

"The Dead End Is Still Worth Seeing" borrows a line from Gerard Manley Hopkins.

ACKNOWLEDGEMENTS

Thank you Kourosh. Your thinking about architecture, playful turns of phrase, and sustaining love opened up the world of these poems.

Thank you Kevin Connolly. I'm so grateful to work on another book with you. Thank you, as well, to everyone at House of Anansi, especially Leslie Joy Ahenda, Lucia Kim, Emma Rhodes, and Greg Tabor. Thank you Bardia Sinaee for copy-editing and making many useful suggestions.

I'm grateful to my friends and family for encouragement, wisdom, and support. Thanks especially to Jean Marc Ah-Sen, Marta Balcewicz, Rebecca Bihn-Wallace, Jake Byrne, Irene Connelly, Suzanna Derewicz, Rene Dhanraj, Stevie Howell, Cody Klippenstein, Mengyin Lin, Christy Luong, Nathan Mader, Guillaume Morissette, Petro Moysaenko, Michael Prior, Abby Seiff, Coby Stephenson, Madeleine Thien, James Yu, Ayesha Wadhawan, André Babyn and Noor Naga for timering, Babak Lakghomi and Khashayar "Kess" Mohammadi for helping with Farsi, and the McFadzean and Fathi families.

Hoa Nguyen's classes on Harryette Mullen and Lorine Niedecker were essential to the thinking and writing of many of the early poems of the book. Anselm Berrigan's class on composition and visual artists inspired many of the later poems.

Thank you to the editors of the following journals, where versions of some of these poems originally appeared: *Afternoon Visitor, American Poetry Journal, Annulet, The Boiler, Columba, The Dalhousie Review, Denver Quarterly, The Drunken Canal, The Fiddlehead, Grain Magazine, Hot Pink, long con, No, Dear,* Pack Animal's *In Heat* pamphlet, *Paperbag, Prelude, Riddle Fence, Tupelo Quarterly, Works & Days,* and *Yalobusha Review.*

I'm grateful to the Canada Council for the Arts, the Ontario Arts Council, and the Access Copyright Foundation for providing essential financial support during the writing of this book.

© Tony Tulathimutte

CASSIDY McFADZEAN studied poetry at the Iowa Writers' Workshop, and fiction at Brooklyn College. She is the author of two books of poetry: *Drolleries* (McClelland & Stewart 2019), shortlisted for the Raymond Souster Award, and *Hacker Packer* (M&S 2015), which won two Saskatchewan Book Awards and was a finalist for the Gerald Lampert Memorial Award. Her crown of sonnets, *Third State of Being*, was published by Gaspereau Press in 2022. She lives in Toronto.